W9-BYZ-751

HUMAN IMPACT ON EARTH: CAUSE AND EFFECT

CHANGING TUNDRA ENVIRONMENTS

ELIZABETH KRAJNIK

PowerKiDS
press
New York

Published in 2020 by The Rosen Publishing Group, Inc.
29 East 21st Street, New York, NY 10010

First Edition

Editor: Jane Katirgis
Book Design: Reann Nye

Photo Credits: Series art Xiebiyun/Shutterstock.com; Alexander Tolstykh/Shutterstock.com; Cafe Racer/Shutterstock.com; cover Gregory A. Pozhvanov/Shutterstock.com; pp. 5, 12 Vadim Nefedoff/Shutterstock.com; p. 6 Adwo/Shutterstock.com; p. 7 Mark Yarchoan/Shutterstokc.com; p. 8 ginger_polina_bublik/Shutterstock.com; p. 9 Evgeny Haritonov/Shutterstock.com; p. 11 Kylie Nicholson/Shutterstock.com; p. 13 Marka/Universal Images Group/Getty Images; p. 14 Natalie B. Fobes/National Geographic Image Collection/Getty Images; p. 15 Andrey Armyagov/Shutterstock.com; p. 16 Roschetzky Photography/Shutterstock.com; p. 17 Kris Grabiec/Shutterstock.com; p. 18 Jeff Zehnder/Shutterstock.com; p. 19 evgenii mitroshin/Shutterstock.com; p. 21 Daniel A. Leifheit/Moment/Getty Images; p. 22 I love photo/Shutterstock.com; p. 23 Kyle T Perry/Shutterstock.com; p. 24 Ronda Kimbrow/Shutterstock.com; p. 25 Carolyn Hebbard/Moment/Getty Images; p. 27 Smith Collection/Gado/Getty Images; p. 28 © Santiago Urquijo/Moment/Getty Images; p. 29 MarcelC/iStock/Getty Images Plus/Getty Images; p. 30 Linda Szeto/Shutterstock.com.

Library of Congress Cataloging-in-Publication Data

Names: Krajnik, Elizabeth, author.
Title: Changing tundra environments / Elizabeth Krajnik.
Description: New York : PowerKids Press, [2020] | Series: Human impact on
  Earth
Identifiers: LCCN 2019003257| ISBN 9781725301405 (pbk.) | ISBN 9781725301429
  (library bound) | ISBN 9781725301412 (6 pack)
Subjects: LCSH: Tundra ecology–Juvenile literature. | Tundras–Juvenile
  literature. | Climatic changes–Juvenile literature. | Nature–Effect of
  human beings on–Juvenile literature.
Classification: LCC QH541.5.T8 K73 2020 | DDC 577.5/86–dc23
LC record available at https://lccn.loc.gov/2019003257

Manufactured in the United States of America

CPSIA Compliance Information: Batch #CSPK19. For Further Information contact Rosen Publishing, New York, New York at 1-800-237-9932.

CONTENTS

WHAT'S A TUNDRA?

Tundra environments are very **unique** places. They cover about one-tenth of Earth's land. The tundra is very cold. It has few life-forms and very simple plants. The very thick soil doesn't drain well, and there is a very short growing season. The tundra contains energy and food in the form of dead plants and animals, and there are large differences in population sizes from one year to the next. There are two types of tundra: arctic tundra and alpine tundra.

However, these environments are undergoing changes that could negatively affect the entire world. Despite being very harsh places, the tundra is very **fragile** and sensitive to change. Global warming is threatening to destroy tundra regions entirely. However, not all hope is lost. Read on to learn how we can repair the damage that has been done.

IMPACT FACTS

"Tundra" comes from the Finnish word *tunturia*, which means "treeless plain." Few trees grow in the tundra, and those that do aren't very tall and don't have very deep root systems.

Even though tundra environments are known for being harsh places, they are also very beautiful. People must do everything possible to protect them.

ARCTIC TUNDRA

The arctic tundra is found in the northern hemisphere from around the North Pole south to the **taiga**. In the arctic tundra, winters are long and cold, and summers are short and cool. The growing season is only about 50 to 60 days. Although the winters are very cold—on average −30°F (−34°C)—the summers are warm enough—around 37 to 54°F (3 to 12°C)—for plants to grow.

PERMAFROST

The arctic tundra is known for its permafrost, or permanently frozen ground. Roots and water can't penetrate, or pass through, it. However, the top layer of the permafrost—called the active layer—thaws each summer, allowing plants to grow. The active layer increases in thickness as you travel farther south in the tundra. When the active layer thaws, water sits on top of the permafrost, creating pools of water.

Because roots can't penetrate the permafrost, tundra plants don't have deep root systems. Instead, their root systems are shallow and grow outward. This also helps them stay rooted during strong winds.

The arctic tundra is home to more than 1,700 **species** of plants. All of these plants are uniquely **adapted** to life there. Most of them have shallow root systems and grow low to the ground. The animals that live in the arctic tundra are also highly adapted to living there. Many have extra fat to keep warm. Others hibernate during the winter months.

ALPINE TUNDRA

Alpine tundra environments are found high in the mountains, mostly in the northern hemisphere. However, alpine tundra environments can be found on mountains throughout the world. They cover about 3 percent of Earth's land. There are no trees in the alpine tundra. But like the arctic tundra, the alpine tundra is known for being covered in snow for a large part of the year. This means the growing season in alpine tundra environments is also short.

IMPACT FACTS

Some plants are only found on the tops of a few mountains. Mountaintops aren't connected and animals may not travel very far from their home range. This means seeds aren't carried to other places.

Lichens are life-forms made of fungi and algae. They grow on rocks and walls, like the ones shown here. They are able to survive in the harsh alpine tundra.

Differences in **elevation** create different habitats for plant and animal life in the alpine tundra. Some plants have special **pigments** to help them better take in light and heat. Plants in the alpine tundra grow very slowly. Animals such as pikas live in alpine tundra environments year-round. Other animals that live there year-round hibernate.

9

WHY IS THE TUNDRA IMPORTANT?

Tundra environments are key to helping scientists track climate change. Permafrost tells them how the earth has thawed throughout history. It also tells scientists how quickly climate change is affecting the tundra right now. Scientists are also able to predict how deep permafrost may be in the future using current measurements and mathematical models.

Arctic tundra environments are commonly known as Earth's carbon sink. This is because the permafrost holds onto much of the world's carbon. This carbon comes from dead plant and animal matter, which is called biomass. The plants of the tundra use the carbon dioxide found in the soil to carry out **photosynthesis**. When the plant dies, they give off carbon dioxide as they decompose, or break down. However, because temperatures are so low in the tundra, this process is very slow.

Very few people live in tundra environments due to the harsh weather and lack of building supplies.

RELEASING CARBON DIOXIDE

Global warming has caused deeper layers of the permafrost to thaw for longer stretches of time. When the soil thaws, biomass decomposes and releases carbon dioxide into the air. Carbon dioxide is a greenhouse gas, and greenhouse gases are what cause global warming. When temperatures are warmer, biomass decomposes even quicker and releases even more carbon dioxide. To stop the permafrost from thawing, we must find ways to lessen the amount of greenhouse gases in the **atmosphere**.

HUMANS AND THE TUNDRA

Even though the tundra is a harsh environment, humans have made their homes there for thousands of years. In North America, people have lived in the tundra since humans crossed the land bridge between Asia and North America, probably more than 14,000 years ago. Over time, these inhabitants have needed food and shelter. So they've taken from the land. They've hunted the animals, built towns and cities, and even begun drilling for oil. Today, about 4 million people live in arctic tundra environments around the world.

MODERN INUIT HOUSING
NUUK, GREENLAND

IMPACT FACTS

The arctic tundra is home to many groups of native people, including the Inuit in Canada, Alaska, and Greenland and the Yu'pik, Iñupiat, and Athabascan in Alaska. In the past, these people lived off of hunting, fishing, and gathering.

The Inuit were once nomadic, which means they moved around a lot to follow their food source. They had to build shelters quickly to protect themselves from the harsh weather. They made snowhouses, which are commonly known as igloos, out of snow blocks.

Human activities, no matter how big or small, can negatively affect tundra life-forms. When humans build their homes or roads, they change the tundra landscape and destroy the homes of plants and animals. The tundra may not bounce back from the damage caused by human activities.

ACTIVITIES AND THEIR CONSEQUENCES

As human populations in the tundra have increased, so have their activities. What began as hunting, fishing, and gathering has now turned to people taking more resources from the tundra than ever before. People have found that the tundra may have large stores of fossil fuels such as crude oil and natural gas. These stores are in the ocean near the tundra.

ARCTIC OIL AND SPILLS

As ice in the arctic thins and melts, ships **transporting** oil can make their way through the water more easily and without icebreakers. However, with this comes the possibility that more oil spills may happen in the arctic. Special bacteria can eat oil if it spills, but the cold temperatures of the arctic may make this type of clean-up harder or impossible. Drilling and transporting oil in the arctic can be very harmful.

Fossil fuels are not renewable energy sources. However, wind energy is renewable and is thought to disturb the arctic environment less.

Drilling for oil can be very harmful to the environment. Spills, leaks, and shipping accidents can hurt plant and animal life. It's impossible to clean up an oil spill completely, and the harsh arctic environment means it will take people longer to get to the spill site. Drilling also disturbs the life-forms that live in arctic environments, such as fish and whales.

GLOBAL WARMING

Human activities beyond the tundra have caused global warming. Our dependence on burning fossil fuels for energy has filled the atmosphere with greenhouse gases. Greenhouse gases trap in some of the heat created by sunlight, the way a greenhouse does. We need the greenhouse effect to keep Earth warm enough for life to exist. However, the more greenhouse gases in the atmosphere, the more heat is trapped.

IMPACT FACTS

Scientists sometimes call global warming "climate change" because different parts of Earth experience global warming differently. Earth's winds and currents move heat around the world, so some places cool off, get warmer, or have more rain or snow.

Global warming has caused habitat loss for a number of tundra species, including polar bears who depend on sea ice for hunting seals.

In the last 300 years, humans have burned more fossil fuels than ever before, creating more greenhouse gases and causing the average global temperature to rise. As the temperature rises, Earth's ice sheets melt and cause sea levels to rise. Global warming can also affect the weather. There may be more severe storms, more rainfall, and drier weather, all of which affects plant and animal life.

As temperatures rise, the unique life-forms living in the tundra may have to move to survive. This is because the life-forms there are highly adapted to that environment. If the environment changes, they need to find a new place that suits them. One example is that tree species adapted to living in very cold temperatures may need to grow farther north or at higher altitudes to continue to survive.

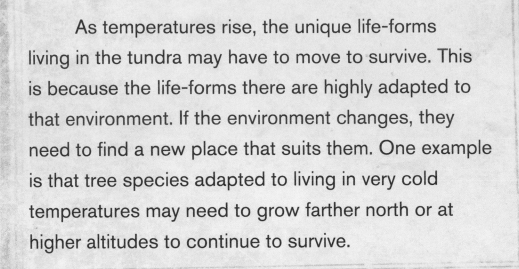

By the year 2050, the tundra may look more like a **coniferous** forest than a treeless plain.

CAN THEY ADAPT?

Some plants and animals may adapt to global warming better than others. However, pollution from burning fossil fuels may harm the delicate species of plants and animals living in the tundra. The animals that eat these life-forms may get very sick or die. One large change we may see in the tundra is taller, woody trees instead of short bushes. However, dark plant life on the ground instead of snow may make global warming worse.

Rising sea levels pose a threat for animals. They also threaten to destroy coastal communities of the tundra. Fishing is part of the way of life for people in many coastal communities. If homes and communities become flooded, people can't continue living in the area. Global warming may also affect fish populations to the point where many species may die out due to warmer ocean temperatures.

WHAT CAN WE DO?

Saving the tundra from global warming and human activities will be a long process. Hundreds of years of damage can't be undone overnight. However, even making small changes can have a positive effect.

One way people can help save the tundra is by depending less on fossil fuels. This needs to happen on a large scale, but large-scale changes can start with just one person. Single-use plastics like to-go cups from coffee shops, utensils from restaurants, and plastic straws are made from fossil fuels. If you'd like to depend less on fossil fuels, use fewer plastic products.

Another way you can help is using less gasoline. If your parents drive you to school each day, you could ride the school bus instead. Or, if you live in a place with nice weather, you could ride your bike to school.

IMPACT FACTS

When the gasoline used in cars and the diesel fuel used in trucks and buses is burned, it creates carbon dioxide. We know this is a greenhouse gas. Using less gas means you're helping save Earth.

In recent years, the population of the Western Arctic herd of caribou in the North American tundra has been declining. To help save these important tundra animals, officials have asked people not to hunt them.

Large-scale changes to lessen our dependence on fossil fuels are necessary to save the tundra and other important environments on Earth. Many power plants use coal as fuel to make electricity. However, this isn't the only fuel out there. Renewable energy sources, such as solar power and wind power, are fairly inexpensive and use far less fossil fuel. Electric cars run off of electricity instead of gasoline and don't burn fossil fuels.

BIOFUELS

Biofuels are plant-based fuel sources. Unlike gasoline and diesel, which come from fossil fuels made from dead plant and animal matter that is millions of years old, biofuels are made from plants grown today. Biofuels can be made from a number different plants including sugarcane and corn. However, when burned, biofuels still create carbon dioxide. The idea behind their benefits is that the plants grown to make the fuel take in just as much carbon dioxide as they create when burned.

Pipelines such as the one pictured here carry fuel to tundra communities, but they can be very harmful if they leak. To prevent damage to the tundra, people shouldn't build more pipelines.

Another way to lessen the effects of global warming is to find ways to take greenhouse gases out of the air. Plants do this naturally. However, when we cut down trees to make room for farmland and cities, all of the carbon those plants stored is released. If we cut down fewer trees and plant more of them, there will be less greenhouse gases in the atmosphere.

STEP CAREFULLY

In the last 20 years, tourism in the tundra has grown very quickly. People like to go to the tundra to see the unique plants and animals that live there. However, this isn't always such a good thing for the plants and animals. The permafrost is very fragile. When cars and trucks are driven on it repeatedly, it can be damaged.

Protect the Tundra
Stay on Paved Trail

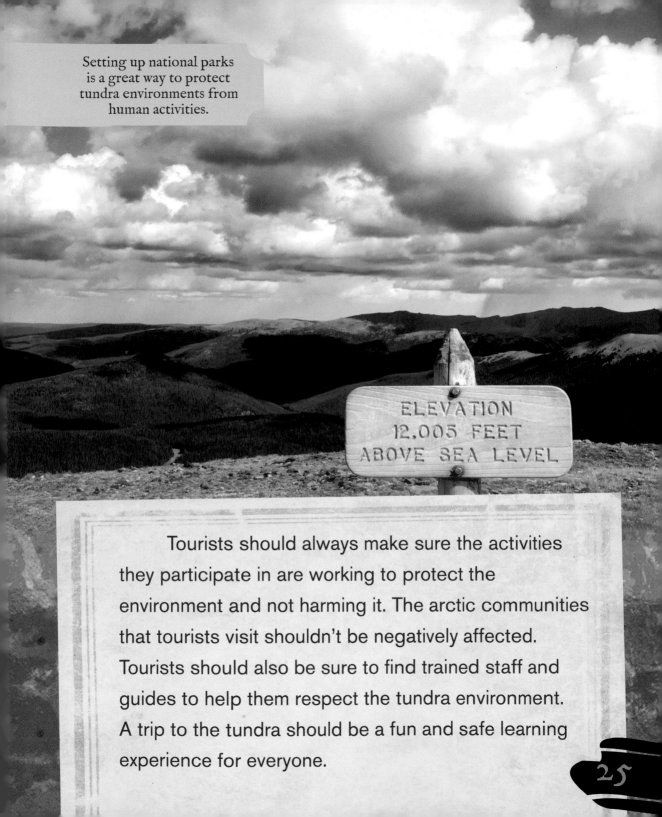

Setting up national parks is a great way to protect tundra environments from human activities.

ELEVATION
12,005 FEET
ABOVE SEA LEVEL

Tourists should always make sure the activities they participate in are working to protect the environment and not harming it. The arctic communities that tourists visit shouldn't be negatively affected. Tourists should also be sure to find trained staff and guides to help them respect the tundra environment. A trip to the tundra should be a fun and safe learning experience for everyone.

Technology today helps us do many things. Scientists use technology to see how tundra environments are changing and to see what they used to be like in the past. One way scientists check on the tundra is to measure permafrost levels. They drill into the soil to see how deep the active layer is, to learn how the soil may have thawed in the past, and to see what the soil is made of.

Scientists in the tundra also take measurements of the snow. Snow acts as a sort of insulation for the ground. The more snow there is, the warmer the ground will be and the more thawing will occur in the permafrost. Continuing to study permafrost levels helps scientists understand how quickly global warming is affecting the tundra.

Here you can see the layers of permafrost that are visible due to water wearing away at the shore. >

To further understand how global warming affects the tundra environment, scientists can also track populations of certain species, such as caribou. They measure the size of the population and follow where the herds migrate. This can help scientists understand where the herd goes and when, which may give them clues about the effects of global warming.

Satellite images of the tundra help scientists understand how much and where thawing takes place. They can also see how much sea ice remains at certain points in the year.

Scientists measure sea ice near tundra regions using **satellite** imagery. This helps them gauge the extent of global warming. Sea ice plays an important part in the health of polar and tundra environments. It lessens coastal erosion caused by waves and protects ice shelves. Sea ice also lessens evaporation and heat loss at the poles. Seals, arctic foxes, and polar bears need sea ice for hunting and lying in the sun.

WHAT'S NEXT?

Not all hope is lost for tundra environments. Scientists are developing renewable energy sources to hopefully replace humans' dependence on fossil fuels. This is one large way we can reverse the damage caused by global warming. As people become more educated about issues like habitat loss and global warming's effects on tundra environments, they become better able to tackle these issues head-on.

Even though you might not be sure how you can help save the environment, there are small changes you can make in your daily life that will help show others how important it is to take care of the environment. Cut down on how many single-use plastics you use each day. Ride your bike to school. It all starts with you!

GLOSSARY

adapt: To change in order to live better in a certain environment.

atmosphere: The whole mass of air that surrounds Earth.

coniferous: Referring to a bush or tree that produces cones and has leaves that are green all year.

elevation: Height above sea level.

fragile: Easily broken or hurt.

photosynthesis: The process by which a green plant turns water and carbon dioxide into food when the plant is exposed to light.

pigment: Natural coloring matter in animals and plants.

satellite: A spacecraft placed in orbit around Earth, a moon, or a planet to collect information or for communication.

species: A group of plants or animals that are all the same kind.

taiga: A wet subarctic forest made up of conifers that begins where the tundra ends.

technology: The way people do something and the tools they use.

transport: To carry from one place to another.

unique: Special or different from anything else.

INDEX

WEBSITES

Due to the changing nature of Internet links, PowerKids Press has developed an
online list of websites related to the subject of this book. This site is updated regularly.
Please use this link to access the list: www.powerkidslinks.com/HIOE/tundra